Close to Home
UNPLUGGED

Close to Home UNPLUGGED

The Second Close to Home Anthology

by John McPherson

Andrews McMeel
Publishing

Kansas City

For Tom

"In loco sporenti abba dabba est."
— James Thurber

Wayne chooses an inappropriate moment to pull the old
"severed-finger in a box" gag.

Bruce activates the new telemarketer-zap
feature on his phone.

Many felt that the company's new dress code was too stringent.

"It can be very dangerous to suppress a hiccup."

"All I need to do is give that cord one good, solid yank and all of the toys are instantly picked up."

In a dramatic sting operation, FBI agents crack down on restaurant employees who don't wash their hands after using the rest room.

Take Your Child to Work Day at Fernview Hospital.

As a convenience to their married customers, some grocery stores have installed cellular phones on their shopping carts.

10

"He must smell your cat."

"It's a reminder from our dentist that your six-month checkup is next Wednesday at two o'clock."

Knowing that there was always bumper-to-bumper traffic at this spot during rush hour, Pete and Chuck established a lucrative partnership.

For the sake of convenience, parents with several children are opting to have in-home pharmacists.

"Oh, those are our wedding photos. We had them all taken using that new 3-D technology!"

"Wait, don't call the plumber yet.
I think I can see the end of the plunger!"

"So far we've been able to heat the entire house
using nothing but junk mail."

"They say if we switch back now, we'll
get twenty-five percent off all calls
made to people with red hair."

14

"I think the satellite dish just blew off the roof."

"How on earth could I have known that your coat was caught on the door handle?"

One of life's unfailing truths: Whenever you pose for a group photo, the others will inevitably choose the photo in which you happen to look like a complete dufus.

After a series of poor performance reviews,
Bob was given a pink slip.

Even though he hadn't asked to have
his hair cut, Dave felt obligated to
pay the street-corner barber.

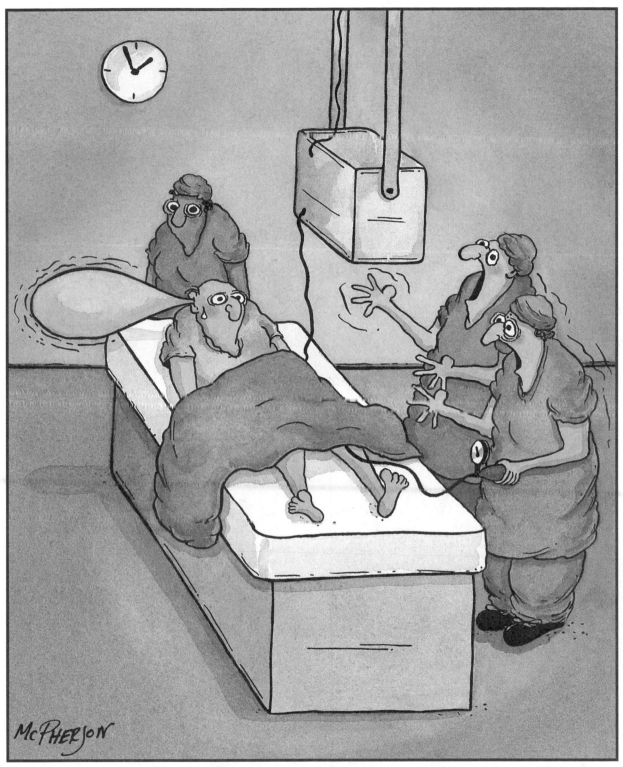

Ted's balloon angioplasty procedure
gets off to a rough start.

"Relax, I know what I'm doing."

"Check and see if the stinger is still in me!"

"You bonehead! That's the same lamp we sold at our garage sale last year for three dollars!"

18

Successful executives know the importance of unwinding after a high-pressure meeting.

... this gold-embossed pacemaker can be yours for the unheard-of price of $19.95! And, if you order now, we'll throw in this Balloon Angioplasty Kit absolutely free! That's right! ...

The Home Shopping Network
expands its product line.

"I need to use the rest room. Hang on to this
end of the rope so I can find my way back."

"You let that cavity go far too long."

"But that's the beauty of it, Rita! I don't have to
worry about my fat intake today. I'm having a
quadruple bypass tomorrow!"

"Be sure to take these with plenty of water."

"I'm starting to think that our early retirement program was a little *too* popular."

"OK, now, Mr. Weston. Let's start by taking care of that tartar build-up."

Andy's dispute with the jerk in 4C heats up.

"Yep, it's beavers, all right. That explains the missing legs to your coffee table."

"OK, fine! If that's the way you wanna play,
I'll make obnoxious gurgling sounds the
next time *you're* putting for birdie!"

"... with anchovies, mushrooms, and extra cheese. Deliver it to 157 Pinehurst. If we're not here, take it to the maternity wing of Glenview Hospital."

"This isn't our house, you idiot!"

24

"Jerry, the claims adjuster is here."

What police officers are actually doing for all that time when they've got you pulled over.

Yet another holiday is created by the gift industry.

Vera ignores the first rule of grocery shopping:
Never shop when you're hungry.

"Unfortunately, Carolyn, your body
has rejected your face lift."

"I heard a loud clunking noise and then
I ran over something large."

To prevent family members from monopolizing
the shower, the Fegleys wisely had the faucet
handles installed outside the bathroom.

"Tom built a dollhouse for the girls
with a full basement."

Hoping to smooth over the heated dispute he had had with Mr. Grant, Ron breaks into the Barney theme song.

"Where the heck did you get this lava lamp, anyway?!"

"Remind me never to play this course again."

"I've got her in one of those new
twenty-four-hour diapers."

Auto-repair shops continue to become
more specialized.

"It's a version of the old shell game. The nurse shuffles the babies around and you bet on which one is yours. So far I've lost forty bucks."

Every once in a while, just for kicks, Dr. Fernlock liked to amplify his drill through the office's stereo system.

"Are you telling me that the only channel we get
is the Weather Channel?!!"

One of many new toys designed to help children
learn more about the real world.

"And how about you, ma'am? Would you like
some ground pepper on your salad?"

Kevin didn't exactly exude confidence when it
came to driving over water hazards.

"Look, it's nothing personal. I just can't handle your cold feet any longer."

"For heaven's sake, Ray! Take a look at this! That mousetrap you set last night has a little doll caught in it that looks just like you!"

Constantly looking for enticing ways to improve its menu, a major pizza chain introduces its new pizza ball.

Fortunately for the rest of the family, the camcorder's boredom sensor kicked in after Dan had spent ten minutes filming the baby sucking on her toe.

THE NATIONAL DAY CARE HALL OF FAME

RYAN BELL
• POTTY TRAINED BY AGE 11 MONTHS
• AVG. NAP TIME, 4½ HRS.

TANYA ZEFF
• GOT DRESSED AND INTO CAR SEAT WITHOUT HELP BY AGE 11 MONTHS

ELLEN HOLT
• STARTED SLEEPING THROUGH THE NIGHT AT AGE 6 DAYS

REGGIE NURBIT
• NEVER CRIED, EVEN WHEN MARBLE GOT STUCK IN NOSE ONE TIME.
• NEVER GOT SICK ONCE.

THE LUXLEY TWINS
• CHANGED EACH OTHER'S DIAPERS BY AGE 13 MONTHS.

AMY KEPPLE
• PREPARED OWN FORMULA AT AGE 5 MONTHS

"These kill seven times as many bugs per hour as bug zappers and use only a third the electricity."

"Hey, Bert. There's a woman here who wants to know if we offer memberships."

Roger would go to any lengths to land this account.

"Unfortunately, Mrs. Dortford, our entire X-ray department is on strike. But if you'll just describe your pain in as much detail as possible, our staff sketch artist should be able to give us a fairly accurate drawing of the problem."

"... and one bottle of extra-potent calcium supplements!"

Despite getting a ten percent discount, Bernice soon regretted allowing the contractor to place his sign in her yard.

"We'd like to ask that the couple sitting behind us be cut off from receiving any more cocktails."

"Ed wanted to make sure that he'd have lots of visitors here, plus it provides a nice supplemental income for the family."

"I still haven't quite gotten used to the clutch on this car."

Another gullible parent is sucked in by pharmaceutical quackery.

Hoover introduces its new vacuum cleaner bags, which, when full, become collectible celebrity replicas.

Management trainee J.K. Boodley tests the boundaries of the company's new dress code.

"We had it installed so we could get a fifteen percent reduction in our fire insurance premium, but we're starting to have a real problem with the dog."

The leading cause of injuries in the home.

Fortunately, Chad was able to intercept his report card just as it was about to fall into the wrong hands.

Thanks to their new garage-sale detector, Norma and Darlene hit a record eleven garage sales in one hour.

"It was George's last request, so I went through with it. But it's making it real tough to find a buyer for the house."

The Litmans' discovery of the tunnel alerted them to an alarming fact: Tippy was leading a double life as someone else's pet.

"This new massage showerhead you installed gives me the creeps!"

With a typical wedding cake costing $300, Ed and Linda opted for the more economical wedding pizza.

"Oh that? That's so I can keep your socks paired up in the laundry."

Thanks to her new personal toddler fence, Janet no longer had to worry about losing track of her kids in crowds.

"They're all out of those paper cones for the cotton candy."

Since it was a gift from Carla, Vern felt obligated to wear his deodorant-on-a-rope to work the next day.

"This diaper service is thirty bucks more a week than any of the others, but it's well worth it."

With final exams in full swing, the administration brought out the cheat-sheet-sniffing dogs.

To help him cope with what was certain to be a tension-filled meeting, Dwight wore his new battery-operated massage shirt.

"Those maniacs up in 4-C are growing watermelons in their window box again this year."

The guys down at Zeffler's Garage were having hours of fun with the remote-control squeal device they had hidden in Mrs. Lambert's car.

"If you get an itch, just turn whichever one of these cranks is closest to it."

Although she had had a few gray hairs in the past, Kay found this one particularly hard to accept.

Nick hoped that the new scope on his driver would put an end to his horrendous slice.

An emerging service industry: wedding truancy officers.

The Bowman Paint Co. needed to work on coming up
with more appealing names for its paint shades.

"Stan?! Bill Wazney wants to know if he
can borrow our fire extinguisher!"

Arnie Slodner had the misfortune of
needing to use the rest room while the flight
attendants were serving beverages.

The First Law of Air Travel: The distance to your connecting gate is directly proportional to the amount of luggage you are carrying and inversely proportional to the amount of time you have.

"I think we better have a little talk with Wilson after the meet."

State troopers along this stretch of I-90 were known for their cunning at catching speeders.

With quality child care becoming tougher to find, many couples are incorporating day-care enrollment into their wedding ceremony.

Chairmaster: for those who want to ease their way into the fitness scene.

"Our idiot veterinarian said that the cat has a serious tartar problem and recommended that I try flossing her teeth!"

"If you paid $5,300 for an exclusive deep-sea fishing excursion and spent the entire time seasick in the bathroom, you'd probably mount the bait bucket, too."

Play-Doh and Toro team up to take snowblower technology to a whole new level.

Bamford county was notorious for its speed traps.

"I hate this hole."

TV viewing changes forever with the innovation of Surround-TV.

"There! I heard it again! There's a mosquito buzzing around here somewhere and *every time* I sit up, it stops!"

Bob was starting to sense that someone in management had it in for him.

"The video is due back at 7 p.m. tomorrow. After that it will begin to emit a hideous stench. Enjoy the movie!"

TLS Industries had a tendency to overmanage its employees.

"Nice break!"

"Poor Muffin! What a nasty hairball that was!"

Another priceless camcorder moment is
destroyed by a loudmouthed stranger.

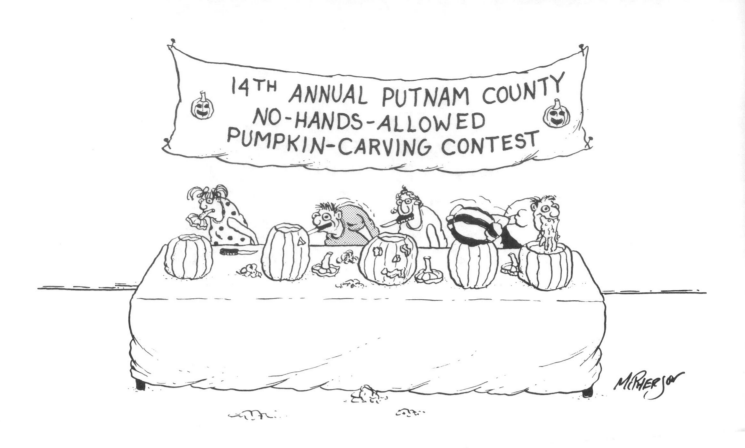

"I've wanted one of those fuzzy toilet-seat covers for years, so for our fortieth anniversary Earl went all out!"

"Well, this is a first. He swallowed one of my gloves!"

"I don't think the chemicals in those flea dips are good for him."

Ray hoped that the stroller would put an end to strangers referring to Jason as a "cute little girl."

Somehow, the big drug-store chains just don't instill the same feeling of confidence that one gets from a neighborhood drug store.

"Will you stop kidding yourself?! You are *not* getting any exercise!"

"Oh, for heaven's sake! This one doesn't feel right either!"

When it got right down to it, nobody had time to spend drying his hands under the new electric hand dryer.

"The doctor says the pin can come out in three months."

Willard Mulnik inadvertently faxes his tie to the Omaha office.

"Unfortunately, ma'am, the fire department can't get here for another two hours. However, a gentleman at the top has volunteered to slide down and try to knock you free."

Vern was starting to sense that Sheila's interest in him was fading.

"These pills come with a child-proof cap, but as an added precaution they're manufactured to look exactly like lima beans."

Having spotted some acquaintances,
Vera activates the instant grandchildren-photo
display on her purse.

It wasn't long before students started to take advantage of
Mrs. Grindle's nearsightedness.

"Oh, hi! I'm Dwayne, your new
upstairs neighbor!"

Although all of the players were given uniforms,
it didn't take long to figure out which guys
weren't going to make the final cut.

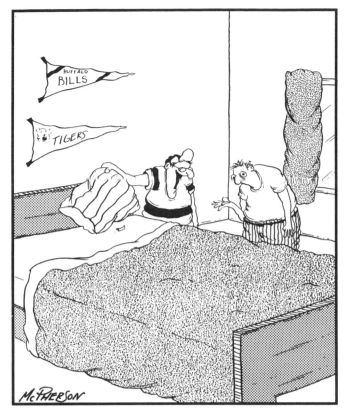

"Relax! There's no way the tooth fairy will figure out that they're dog teeth!"

To help customers fit into the bathing suits they wanted, Felman's Department Store wisely installed stair-stepping machines in its women's department.

Desperate people do desperate things.

"And what seems to be the problem with the shampoo, ma'am?"

"And here are the keys to the car."

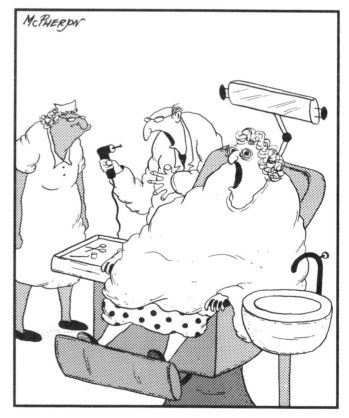

"Unbelievable! What are the chances of *three* drill bits snapping off in a row like that?!"

"All I did was hit the delete button!"

Edwin's new Eau de Hershey Bar cologne was having a dramatic effect on his love life.

"So, to make a long story short, the insurance company tells us in the midst of it all that it'll pay for only half of the liposuction."

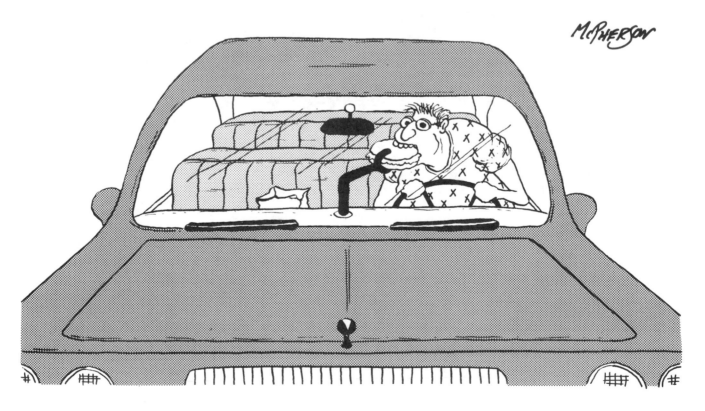

Catering to customers who frequent drive-thru restaurants, some car manufacturers are installing driver's side burger clips.

"The in-flight movie is four dollars. If you're not interested in the movie, we ask that you wear one of these masks until the film is over."

With any luck, maintenance would take the hint and turn down the air conditioning.

"According to the instructions, we can't drive faster than three miles per hour or have a total passenger weight over 150 pounds while the spare is being used."

Company chairman Lloyd Fegman didn't have much patience for what he considered to be dumb questions.

The Wassermans discover that the air bags in their new car are a tad on the sensitive side.

"Cotton candy? You traded your *glove* for some cotton candy?!!"

Although no one at the table had said a word about it, Doug and Sandy sensed that they were being fixed up.

"For heaven's sake! If it's that big a deal to you, let's get cable!"

"Hold still! I want to use up these last few shots on the roll!"

"Personally, I think it's cruel to make the poor
things walk all that way through the tube,
but Gene likes to see them up close."

"OK, hit the button!"

"We have no idea what you have, Mr. Schaad, but whatever it is, it's extremely contagious."

"Look, I don't have a cent in the car. Here are four Chiclets and a ticket to my son's high school play."

"Hold it! Nobody move! I just lost a contact!"

"The moles have been just *awful* this year!"

"I need everything except this for a '92 Ford Taurus."

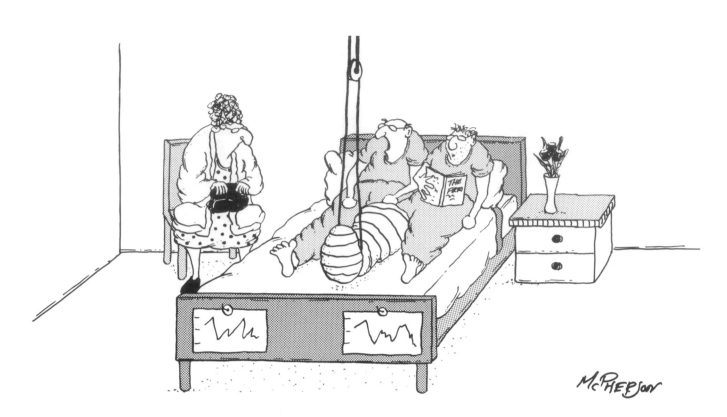

"I know I asked for an economy room, but this is ridiculous."

The Puzney High Wombats are undefeated since they got their new uniforms.

"What kind of an idiot drinks three cups of coffee after 9 p.m.?!"

A good indication that the softball league
you've joined isn't overly competitive.

"Oh, I forgot to tell you. I let the kids take the spare tire to play with in the sandbox."

As a service to health-conscious customers, many grocery stores have installed scanners that calculate the total number of calories purchased.

"Something tells me the dog resents having been trained to retrieve the paper."

In an attempt to get their patients to relax more, many dentists have installed Jacuzzis in their offices.

By tapping into the stabilizing power of gyroscopes, Wade was able to teach his son to walk at just five months.

Vera's desire to slim down for her honeymoon was turning into a full-scale obsession.

After hearing that electric blankets emit harmful electromagnetic waves, Norm and Sheila switched to a wood-fired blanket.

"They're *perfect,* Charles! I'll think of you every time I wear them."

"For heaven's sake! All he wants to do is play horsey with his dad! Will you stop whimpering and at least *try* to jump over the coffee table?!"

In a play unprecedented in league history, Ned Felmley misreads the third-base coach's signals and steals the pitcher's mound.

"Because, Mr. Westcott, your insurance doesn't cover the cost of a hospital room after gall bladder surgery."

TAN-B-GONE

1761

REPLACE THAT BEAUTIFUL BRONZE GLOW WITH A SICKLY, PALLID LOOK IN JUST 15 MINUTES!

A new service for people who call in sick and spend the day playing in the sun.

To help boost the morale of employees in windowless offices, Voltech Industries installed TV monitors displaying live footage of a nearby window.

"We gotta stop feeding the dog dry food."

Having narrowed the field of candidates to three, personnel goes through the final selection process.

It dawned on Carol that today was the day the realtor had said he wanted to show the house.

Without a doubt, one of the all-time worst places to get a flat.

"That goofball over there offered me five bucks to put this helmet on his kid long enough to get a photo."

"Our dryer's broken."

"Go get the phone number of those idiots who
installed the vinyl siding."

"I'm sorry, sir, but leg room is no longer a
service that we offer to our coach passengers."

Nobody was too pleased with the
yearbook staff at Whatney High.

Dwayne made a mental note to change the filter in the furnace.

Day-care centers are becoming increasingly selective about which students they admit for enrollment.

Wendy and Charlene were pretty impressed with Ed's surfing abilities until the tide receded.

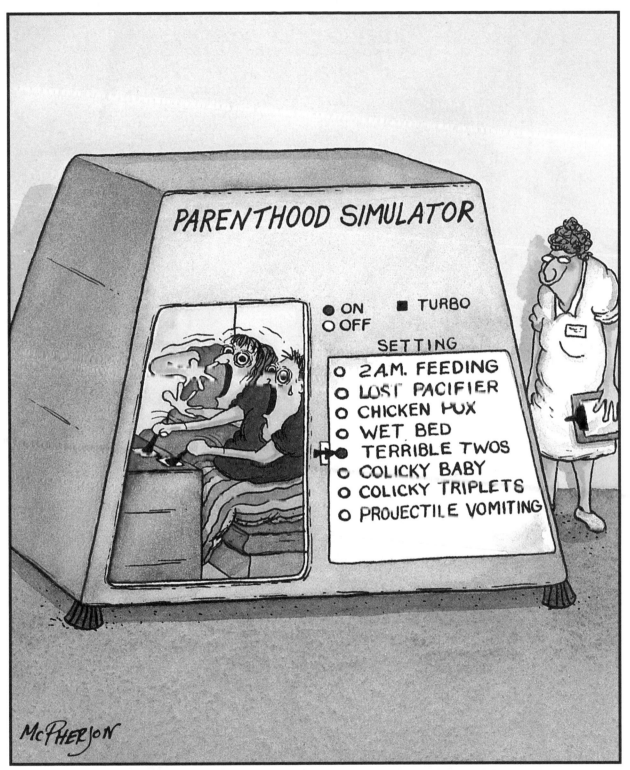

In an effort to prepare expectant parents for the challenges that lie ahead, many obstetricians' offices have installed parenthood simulators.

When wedding photographers abuse their power.

The management of Chandler Industries didn't have much tact when it came to layoffs.

"Well, sure, honey, I'll take another cup of your tea. That's very sweet of you."

Sheila had an effective way of letting telemarketers know she wasn't interested.

"For $1,800 I expected our home security system to be a little more sophisticated than this!"

Carl wore the slippers for two weeks until one day they had an unfortunate "accident" involving the garbage disposal.

"Nuts! I think we're going to need an adapter for this."

"It's a free trial-size sample of cat litter."

"Well, your lawn's all set, Mrs. Fertstein! Here are some hermetically sealed protective suits and some respirators in case someone actually needs to walk on the lawn this summer."

"If you ask me, the neighbors are abusing this new leash law."

"He fell while he was trying to install some of those nonslip decals in the tub."

Having just learned that she won the lottery, hair stylist Ramona Yotz has a little fun with the one customer who failed to tip her in twelve years.

"We apologize if we startled you, folks. However, state law requires that we perform unannounced Heimlich maneuver drills once every month."

"Don't clench your fist quite so hard."

"Well, look on the bright side. It's the only weed in the whole yard."

93

"Don't play with your food, dear."

Ed Mosberg's cannonball would go down
in Pulver Country Club history.

As the last item was being rung up, Alan realized
he had shopped with a list that had been lying in
the cart, not the one his wife had given him.

Although she had endured many horrendous gas-station rest rooms, Susan had a feeling that this one would go down in infamy.

"Okee-doke! Let's just double-check. We're 130 feet up and we've got 45 yards of bungee cord, that's uh   90 feet. Allow for 30 feet of stretching, that gives us a total of . . . 120 feet. Perfect!"

"Does anybody have a one-inch hex nut?!!"

"He's at the stage now where everything he gets his hands on goes straight into his mouth."

Some of the rides at the Fernvale county fair
left a lot to be desired.

"Do you want to be the one to go outside when it's minus-fifteen
to get some firewood? All right then, quit complaining!"

"I'm sick of stubbing my toe on this doorway."

Just minutes into their shopping spree,
Jean and Lisa are ambushed by a gang
of hostile cosmetic clerks.

"I was under the impression that it was the *restaurant* that revolved."

It didn't take much to upset Mrs. Stegler.

"It's a merry-go-round for kids who don't get to spend enough time with their dads."

It was several weeks before the Millsville Department of Public Works realized that it had mistakenly purchased a Zamboni rather than a street cleaner.

"Are you nuts?! Who in his right mind tries out a jet ski in a backyard swimming pool?!!"

"For twenty-five bucks I'll shovel a path to your snow blower."

Every graduate's deepest fear.

"Those morons downstairs got their kid a model rocket kit."

"Unfortunately, ma'am, our fitting rooms are being renovated. But if you'll just step behind this clothing rack, Belly and Rowena will be happy to stand guard for you while you change."

"You rode your bike to work again, didn't you?"

"Calm down, Lois! You're getting all worked up over nothing! Look at the shape of its head! That snake's not poisonous!"

102

"Your root canal is pretty straightforward, Mrs. Zagler, so I'm going to turn things over to the Auto-Dentist. If you have any problems, just pull on that cord above your head."

Hoping to bolster its sagging ticket sales, Comet Airlines introduces its new line of glass-bottomed jets.

"We've made some revisions in our retirement program. In lieu of a pension, you'll now get one limited-edition Elvis collector's plate per pay period."

"Frank, Doug Parsons wants to know if you can help put up Christmas lights on the big spruce tree in their front yard."

"Wait a second, Don! It's not broken! My knee had just loosened the plug! See?! It's working fine now!"

"OK, listen *very* carefully. Take this pill. If you start to feel numbness in your legs or have trouble pronouncing vowels, pull it out immediately."

Clarice was having a difficult time accepting the fact that she was no longer a size 8.

"Is this National Farm Insurance? I need $200,000 of tornado insurance! Make it effective right now! Here's my credit card number!"

"I got sick of cleaning up hairballs."

"For the third time, sir, there are *no* other seats available! Now please take your seat."

"That's nothin'! *I've* got a friend who was in labor for sixty-seven hours, she couldn't take any medication because she's allergic, and in the midst of it all the entire maternity staff went on strike and her baby had to be delivered by a janitor."

"Well, we found out what was causing that squealing noise. Your wife had been sitting on a tack."

**The new breed of insensitive friends:
people who call during *Seinfeld*.**

"I'm sorry, sir, but there's a four dollar fee for asking questions."

"By adding a new 120-megabyte hard drive and using the software that Ed developed over the last six months, we can compute anybody's handicap to within 1/1,000th of a stroke."

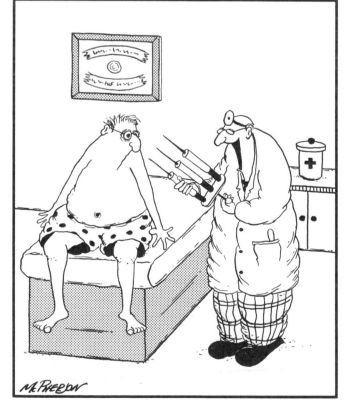

"Fortunately, medical researchers have been able to combine tetanus, smallpox and rubella vaccinations into one shot."

A sense of apathy was beginning to creep into the company's employee-of-the-month program.

What not to say to your wife
when she's in labor.

The Second Law of Grocery Shopping:
If you shop for just a few items using one of
the shopping baskets, you will inevitably
find thirty or forty other items you need.

Karl takes the concept of vanity plates to
previously unknown levels of narcissism.

"Will you stop whining? I told you three times that this restaurant
requires men to wear a jacket and tie!"

"If you start to feel dizzy or weak,
get outside immediately. Your new
pacemaker is solar-powered."

"Ever since we had the grease fire in the kitchen,
George has been a bit overprotective."

Virgil's new litterbox-emptying device
worked great until his neighbors down in 4B
returned from their three-week vacation.

As soon as Mrs. Felster began to read the minutes of the last meeting, the board members knew she was not going to work out as the new secretary.

Virgil's new Sippy-Cup Body Straw was the perfect way to cool off on a hot day

"I can't believe I locked myself out again. Thank heavens for these clever hide-a-keys!"

Gary was beginning to have some concerns
about his new group health plan.

"I don't think you understand! I said, the pacifier
fell out somewhere back in the airport! Tell the
pilot to turn the plane around—now!"

"I had trouble reading your doctor's handwriting, but I think I figured it out. However, if you start to drool uncontrollably or gain more than fifteen pounds in a week, stop taking them."

The Thuckleys couldn't help but be jealous of the Furmans' new all-terrain stroller.

"Thank heavens the plumber knows CPR!"

YOU HAVE REACHED DEBBIE WILMER BABYSITTING, INCORPORATED. FOR RESERVATIONS, PRESS 1. FOR ACCOUNTING, PRESS 2. FOR RESEARCH AND DEVELOPMENT, PRESS 3. TO SPEAK TO MS. WILMER'S PERSONAL SECRETARY, PRESS 4.

A clear sign that your baby sitter is becoming too popular.

"This one's got a stopwatch, lap counter, and is
waterproof to a depth of 100 feet."

"Sorry, sir, we're out of boxes."

"It certainly is an enthusiastic staff."

"If they come after you, try to run this direction so I can get it on video."

"Yep, here it is right here. Your extended warranty covers only the glove compartment, dome light, and vanity mirror."

"And . . . uh . . . how about your . . . uh . . . sideburns? Do you want them trimmed, too?"

"Good news! The exploratory surgery
turned up negative!"

"I accidentally dropped my gum into the money canister. Would you mind returning it with my cash?"

"That Novocain should wear off in two or three days."

THE CREATURE THAT LURKED IN THE CLOSET NO MATTER HOW MANY TIMES DADDY CHECKED AND SAID IT WASN'T THERE

"This new choir director certainly has spunk."

Thanks to the wonders of virtual reality, fathers can now completely experience the miracle of giving birth.

"That suit is called 'The Optical Illusion.'"

The personnel department at Carner Industries was known for its impersonal interviewing process.

"We finally got smart and had speed bumps installed."

In a cruel twist of fate, the Bowmans discover that they live between the Publishers Clearing House Grand Prize and First Prize winners.

"Unfortunately, Mr. Mendrick, your insurance doesn't cover some of the more conventional hearing aids."

"Here's your allowance. You're free to do with it as you please, but I strongly recommend that you put twenty-five percent of it away for retirement."

"Don finally figured out a way to keep the squirrels from getting at the bird feeder."

"I think your serve would improve significantly if you'd just get that thing restrung."

"I'll be happy to cash your check, Mr. Gleckman, but first I'll need twenty-three forms of ID, ten letters of reference, and a sample of your blood."

"The earpiece on the phone was starting to look pretty gross."

Most employees found that playing the new game in the cafeteria was a great way to relieve stress.

"Kathy! Kathy! Snap out of it! Your aerobics show has been over for twenty minutes! That's 'Mister Rogers' Neighborhood' you're watching!"

Warren makes a last-ditch effort to start his mower.

"Dr. Bickford is trying out a new inoculation method he found out about when he was traveling in Borneo."

"Claudia, you've come to the right place. Our firm specializes in hair salon malpractice suits."

Knowing that wedding receiving lines are notorious for being dull,
Pete and Gloria did their best to liven theirs up.

"This? Oh, nothing. It's just a radio-transmitter collar so Lisa's dad can track you down if you don't get her home by midnight. No big deal."

"We ran out of IV bags."

"Good evening, sir! I was on my way to the video store and realized I forgot to rewind the tape. Mind if I use your VCR?"

"For heaven's sake! We better use the SPF 45 today!"

MASTER LAMAZE IN JUST 10 MINUTES

"You've got two options. You can wait until a technician from the escalator company flies in here on Monday, or we can start it up and hope that you come out at the top."

"Mrs. Nortman just sent in this fax of a rash that she's got on her stomach."

"'Next, attach shunt C to rod F.' ... Hey, wait! These are the assembly instructions for the kids' swing set, not the tent."

"Buying that mirror from the funhouse was the smartest thing we ever did."

Thanks to Muffin, Karl hadn't had to shampoo his hair in two-and-a-half years.

". . . and this is Miney, and this is Mo."

Although the other employees adored him, Wayne the stockboy had a dark side.

At The National Academy of Mall Security Guards.

"So, how's the rototilling going, Mr. I-Don't Need-to-Read-the Directions?"

Many top-of-the-line fitness machines now come equipped with a motivational alarm that sounds if the machine is not used for at least twenty minutes a day.

At the Hair Club for Men quality-control center.

"Good afternoon, sir. My name is Daryl, and I'll be your ticketing officer."

Management at the Zebco Novelty Co. continued to be puzzled by the company's declining productivity.

"I jerked the wheel hard to the left to avoid hitting the squirrel, and then I heard this horrible twisting noise."

"Hal and I used to get devoured by mosquitoes, but since we started wearing the bat houses, we haven't had a single bite."

"The salesman said that these provide three times the traction of regular golf shoes!"

"Does this sweater make me look bulky?"

The latest innovation in air travel: convertible jets.

"All right! All right! You've made your point, Dad!
I'll get rid of my earring, I swear!"

"In addition to the stereo, this one's also got AC."

"Management says they're fed up with losing foul
balls and homers to the fans."

137

"It's all yours!"

Before going out on a blind date,
Claudia always checks out the guy thoroughly
with her Weirdometer.

Late in the day, when all of the popular videos have been rented, they appear:
video scavengers who prey on customers returning videos.

"The baby is four months, Jason is seventeen months,
and Lisa is 147 months."

"If you don't mind, Mr. Morris, I'd like to get one more photo with you, me, and some of the ambulance attendants, and then we'll get you right over to X-ray."

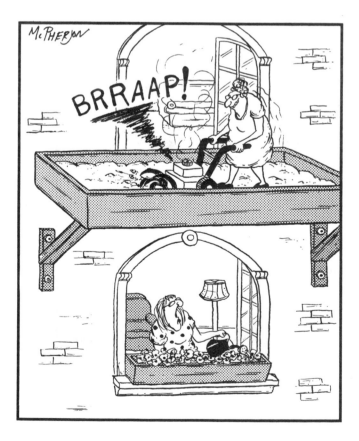

BRRAAP!

"Oh, LASER. Well, I'm sorry, but that still looks like an 'O' on your application to me."

"Us? We're fine! Bill had surgery on his lower back last month, but other than that, life's been pretty uneventful."

"It's one of the new easy-open twist-off caps."

To help provide even speedier service to their customers, many fast-food restaurants have begun to employ psychics.

Rather than risk biting into a chocolate that
she didn't like, Barb pulled out her
creme-filling detector.

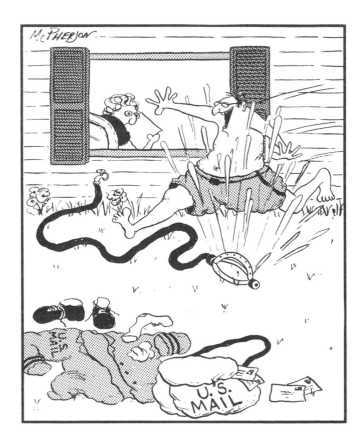

Although no one could quite put a finger on it,
there was something strangely unnerving
about the new biology teacher.

To discourage himself from using his credit card, Ray got into the habit of duct-taping it to his stomach.

"So much for our security deposit."

"You've probably noticed that we're in the midst of a power outage here."

The city's new parking meters, which spew hot tar onto cars whose time has expired, proved to be highly effective battling scofflaws.

The Wickman family did its best to make the usually dull task of detrimming the tree more lively

"Hey, listen to this! According to the scorecard, this golf course was designed by Stephen King!"

Overzealous parents continue to be a problem at
Little League parks throughout the country.

"Now *this* is what I call an ice storm!"

"Let me see the cruise brochure again!"

Some shoppers felt that Zippy Grocery Stores
had gone too far with this latest
offering of free samples.

"Please put down the photo of
Cindy Crawford, ma'am."

The humiliating moment when you realize that the church
program said to sing verses one, two, and three, but not four.

"There you go, sir."

"This new attachment I got makes ironing shirts a piece of cake."

"Comstock's moving a little slow on that Megatron Industries proposal. Give him seventy-five volts for five seconds. What the heck, make that ten seconds."

Raymond tries out his new sweat-diverting eaves trough

Jerry could almost taste the sale.

"It's Stephen King's latest book in extra-large type."

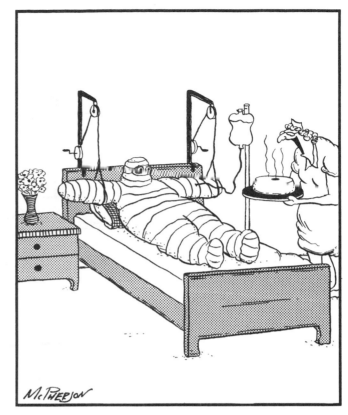

"Here you go! T-bone steak, mashed potatoes, and fresh asparagus! Whoops! What am I doing? This is for Mr. Cagner in room 173."

THE RELATIVES OF ED + SUE VOSBURG TOTALLY UNANNOUNCED TOUR

"Oh, that? That's my new automatic lawn-mowing system.
Step over here and I'll show you how it works."

"How about you, sir: Would you like the
house wine also?"

SOUTHPOINT CHIROPRACTIC CENTER

CRACK!

No one could guess gifts like Jean Morrissey.

"The plumber says that the replacement parts for the toilet won't be in for three more weeks, and he left us this."

"A Barbie doll got stuck under the brake pedal."

FELINE EYE CHART

SOUTHVILLE VETERINARY CENTER

"All right, Mrs. Clandell. Cover Muffin's right eye."

"I don't care if you're sentimental! We need a new mattress!"

More and more businesses are teaming up
with airlines to offer frequent-flier miles
to their customers.

Talking scales: Proof that technology
isn't always good.

Hugh tries out his new Swiss Army Golf Clubs.

"Take the entire bottle of pills immediately!"

"He's a real lap cat, that one is!"

"Those are 100 percent turkey feathers! They never need painting, have ten times the R-value of vinyl siding, and not a single tree had to be cut down!"

"He says he's thirsty."

Attempts to make the church newsletter more exciting were getting out of hand.

"*Independence Day* wasn't available, but I found something I think you'll like even better. It's a Lithuanian film with Tibetan subtitles."

"My dog ate it."

The latest technology in the quest for faster pizza delivery.

"The actual parts for your exhaust system weren't available, but we were able to modify some parts we had in stock."

Comet Airlines revolutionizes the airline industry
by offering ultra-super-duper first class.

Lyle liked to think of himself as a
full-service waiter.

Tensions mounted in the office as a gang of
IBM users strayed into the Mac users' turf.

"Since when did they start alphabetizing grocery stores?"

"Excuse me, folks, can we squeeze by?"

Aunt Ruth had a knack for getting children gifts that their parents hated.

"Oh, my! This is *much* worse than I thought! I'm afraid we may have to pull *all* of these lower teeth! Take a look and see if you agree, Ms. Comstock."

Fortunately for Donna and Clarice, Food Wizard had the foresight to install airbags in its shopping carts.

A typical group photo taken with an auto-timer.

The Nilburns stumble onto the Secret Toddler Treasure Trove.

"It's your turn to empty the litter box."

The pressure of the SAT finally pushes
Brian Folbert over the edge.

"Our sneeze guard is out for repairs.
Would you mind wearing this helmet?"

"Let's put it on high for twenty minutes. She's gotta fall asleep after that."

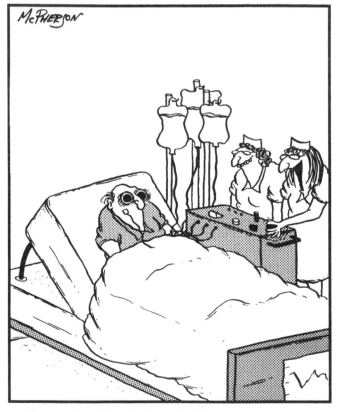

"Hey, Carol! Look how big his eyes get when
you turn this blue dial *way* up!"

Due to recent cutbacks, several major airlines have eliminated their snack carts.

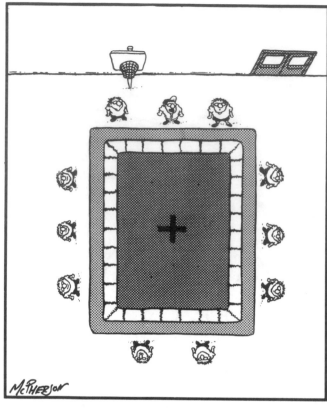

"Let go of the ceiling, Wilkins!"

"I know every man needs to have a hobby, but this is really starting to grate on me."

"Well, Brad, now that we both agree you deserve a raise, what do you say we make things interesting?"

Vern was beginning to have some doubts about the builder he had selected.

"Two more records to go and I'll have logged every single item we own for our insurance records."

"We're not sure what this thing is, but we took it out and your car seems to be running a lot smoother."

"The salesman said this is a state-of-the-art model that doesn't need a remote."

"Some joker sprayed the melons again with that hair-in-a-can stuff."

With 150 miles to go and fatigue setting in, Alan wisely turned on his anti-drowsiness device.

"Honestly! The 3-D effect in these video games is incredible!"

"Before we begin today's dissection lab, I'd like you each to select your lab specimen and take it back to your lab table."

"It only takes Susan B. Anthony dollars!"

When dieting goes too far.

In an incredible stroke of luck, Brian discovers that the Final Jeopardy question is the same as the twenty-point bonus question on his take-home midterm.

"This workout tape's a little more laid-back than
some of the others."

The latest in family health care:
infection detectors.

The Lampleys discovered a simple way to pass the food during Christmas dinner.

"Remind me never to ask the youth group to help fold the church bulletins again."

"Ray? It's Vern. The computers are down again."

The Candle Glow Inn introduces its new scratch-and-sniff menus.

After four hours of lugging a twenty-eight–pound toddler around a mall, Doug is stricken by a case of Baby-Backpack Syndrome.

The Sunday *Bugle Herald* adapts a popular children's book feature and introduces pop-up personal ads.

"Quick! Put this Nixon mask on the Simkins baby! His father's coming down the hall!"

"Could I please have six or seven extra air-sickness bags?"

"That's it, Wade! You've got him! Tighten up on the line a bit! Perfect! You're wearin' him down! . . ."

"Now's the part where you're supposed to say, 'The important thing is that you're OK, son.' Give it a try, Dad. Eight simple words."

"Will you quit whining?! You're the one who wanted real maple syrup."

"What kind of an idiot hires two seventh-graders to install vinyl siding?!"

A hideous new fad: 3-D tattoos.

"For heaven's sake, Frank, this is no time to
be a hero! Give them what they want!
You've got a family to think about!"

Charlene took the business of screening prospective roommates very seriously.

Another case of carpool abuse.

"Whoa! Hold up, I think we goofed. She's in for an appendectomy."

Wayne's .026 batting average was well-known throughout the league.

"Let me know if you find a set of dentures in there, ma'am."

"Mr. Farnsley, I haven't got the slightest idea what song you're humming. Please take the stethoscope out of your mouth so we can finish your examination."

The Wilsons and the Fegleys quickly regretted paying twenty bucks extra for a room with a view.

CHUCK'S AUTOMATIC CAR WASH

"And you're *sure* you had the door when you entered?"

**Darren decides to get the roll-bar option
on his in-line skates.**

"When was the last time we dusted around here?"

Kevin finally found a way to keep his
head down when he swings.

ALVIN KRONK, M.D.
EYE, EAR, NOSE,
AND THROAT.

LOUIS VARBER, M.D.
HEAD, SHOULDERS,
KNEES AND TOES,
KNEES AND TOES.

"It's a deodorant holder! This way you can put deodorant on both underarms at the same time!"

"He's half black Lab and half Siberian husky."

Murphy's Law of New Shirts: No matter how many pins you remove from a new shirt, there's always one more.

Ultra-sensitive car alarms.

"That new kid at the pizza shop is starting to get on my nerves."

Larry had been getting increasingly apathetic about walking the dog.

SCRACK!

"That 'jerk' that keeps trying to pass us is our trailer."

"Which do you want? Fudge Royale or Neapolitan?"

How the IRS really decides
whose return gets audited.

"Good news, Warren! The airbags in the new car work perfectly!"

More and more students are turning to private coaching firms to help them score higher on the SAT.

Bud Wellman discovers the true value of a self-propelled lawn mower.

"If it bothers you, tell him to put his feet down!
Otherwise, quit whining to me about it!"

After the slide projector broke,
Dave's presentation to the board of directors
took a drastic turn for the worse.

"All right! All right! We can get a dishwasher!"

Dan just wasn't working out as a spotter for the gymnastics team.

"Bernice? Glenda Pratner up in 27-B. Hey, take a look out your dining room window and see if my air conditioner is hanging nearby and try to haul it inside."

In recent years, many companies have found it necessary to employ Game Police.

THE GAP

"While you're at it, get me a cheeseburger,
a large order of fries, and a chocolate shake."

Hoping to appeal to both performance-minded dads and practical moms,
Chevrolet develops the Corvette minivan.

"Worst slice I ever saw!"

By tattooing employees each time they take a sick day, Feckley Industries
has been able to dramatically reduce sick leave abuse.

Don and Ellen Finley attempt to leave their
four-month-old with a sitter for the first time.

"Oh, walt! I think I found the problem!
I've been using the Nebraska map instead
of the Vermont map!"

"I'm sorry, ma'am, but I'm afraid your husband
doesn't qualify as a carry-on item."

"Children or non-children?"

Knowing that he was about to be fired, Vern took the company car out for one last spin.

Functional as well as elegant, No-pest earrings are becoming quite the rage.

After the seventh consecutive viewing of *Barney Goes to Cleveland*, Alan suffers a spontaneous boredom attack.

Unfortunately, Arnie's trick with the bubble gum
did little to impress his interviewer.

Twenty-seven weeks on the all-radish diet finally pushed Carolyn over the edge.

Deep down inside, Coach Knott had always wanted to be a math teacher.

"This way, if I wipe out, I'll roll instead of getting scuffed up."

"Who would've thought that a car this size could fit underneath a tractor trailer?!"

"I videotaped my jogging route so that on rainy days all I need to do is start the tape and run on the treadmill until I see our driveway."

A definite sign that you'll be waiting for your doctor's appointment much longer than expected.

"I am not *wearing* stockings, thank you!"

Thanks to her new blanket security system,
Mary Ann was able to thwart Jim's
attempts to steal the blanket.

"There must've been a hundred signs! 'Don't Feed the Bears!' So what do you?! You start handing cookies to them!"

Dwight was having a difficult time accepting the fact that summer was over.

Lois Mulner wanted to make sure nobody walked off with her bag by mistake.

"The plumber said he ran into some unexpected problems and will be back sometime next week."

"Something tells me that the guy in the room above me isn't doing so well."

"Hey, kid. I'll give you five bucks if you'll crawl around in there, find a little boy with a red-striped shirt and bring him out."

Larry Vulmer: the Comb-Over King.

BOB'S LIST

☒ MOW THE LAWN
☒ PAINT ENTIRE HOUSE
☐ GET RID OF SQUIRREL CARCASS IN CRAWL-SPACE
☐ BUILD DECK
☐ SEEK AND DESTROY NOXIO SMELL IN LAUNDRY ROOM
☐ CAULK ATTIC TO KEEP BATS OUT
☐ REMOVE TICKS FROM DOG

"Are you *serious*?! She won't let you take off the shirt until *all* of those chores are done?!"

The trend in the '90s is toward
highly specialized colleges.

"We had child safety gates built into the house.
The collar Jason is wearing activates the gate
anytime he gets within ten feet of the stairs."

"We're in luck, Dave! I found my Triple-A card!"

Mrs. Lasky hoped that oral midterms in
Spanish 201 would give students a
unique cultural experience.

"I've seen unusual rashes before, but this is incredible! There's Fiji, and New Guinea! Look!
You can even see snow on top of Mount Everest!"

"I just clocked you doin' 127 miles an hour!
You've got some explainin' to do, mister!"

MAPS OF DOG-LESS
JOGGING ROUTES
$5

"Could you go over the part about the
seat belts one more time?"

"For her twelve years of service as a data processor and for keypunching in 3,789 records in one eight-hour shift, please welcome our employee of the year, Peggy Neal!"

"That wisdom tooth on the right side was giving me a tough time. So I had to get at it from a different angle."

"When the guy at the front desk told us there was a bar in our room, this wasn't what I had in mind."

"Hey, I agree with you! They did a great job cleaning the carpets.
I just think they should've asked before they stenciled their logo on the rug!"

Bobby's excitement about going to summer camp
faded as soon as he read the sign.

"Here's one that says 'Pat Frawley' on it.
Pat Frawley hasn't worked here since 1987!"

"I'm Carla and this is my friend Rose."

"We should've bought one of those cardboard shades to put on the dashboard."

"We need to put more chlorine in the pool. I think I see some algae growing here."

"Hi! We're the Litmans! We tried to rent *Jurassic Park* but were told
that you folks got the last copy. Mind if we watch it with you?"

"Take one of these every time you inhale."

Accurately ordering mulch by the cubic
yard is a skill that few people possess.

For those difficult bedtimes,
Sheryl relied on the bedtime reel.

"I rigged up the phone so you can talk
while you're cooking."

"Well, it's hard to say from here, but my guess is your vertical hold is shot."

As someone who can never remember names, Roger relied on his new Insta-Name to bail him out of awkward social situations.

The real reason Al Brimlow bought a mulching mower.

For people who can't afford a minivan, elastic trunk lids
are proving to be an inexpensive alternative.

"Well now, Mr. Fenderson, what
seems to be the problem?"

"I just figured, hey, why spend a fortune on a set
of yuppie-looking wrist and ankle weights?"

"Here's today's special: braised beef medallions in a sherry sauce. I'm sure this kind gentleman won't mind if you all sample a bite."

"According to the map, there should be a traffic circle coming up."

Dwayne was starting to reconsider his decision to be water boy for the cross-country team.

LUGGAGE COMPACTOR TS-4900

KACHUNG!

"I never heard of someone having salmon as pets."

"Unfortunately, ma'am, this airplane is not equipped with rest rooms. We do, however, have this personal lavatory and a privacy blanket for your convenience."

Unable to afford bells for a bell choir, members of the Maple Valley Church improvised as best they could.

"Folks, we're going to give an old tradition a
new twist. Rather than throw the bride's bouquet,
we're going to open the gate and see which
one of you lucky single gals can snatch the
bouquet from old Cyclone here!"

The Wormsleys had had one too many milkshakes spilled on their new cloth seats.

How to tell when it's time to
clean up your driveway.

At the Department of Motor Vehicles
Employee Training Center.

This incident, involving the neighbors' Sunday
Times Herald, forced Lois to admit that she
had a coupon-clipping addiction.

The staff at Wilmont obstetrics just couldn't resist
pulling the fake sonogram trick.